College is Yours
IN 600 WORDS OR LESS

BY PATRICK J. O'CONNOR

Outskirts Press, Inc.
Denver, Colorado

College is Yours in 600 Words or Less

Patrick J. O'Connor, Ph.D.

Outskirts Press, Inc.
10940 South Parker Road - 515
Parker, CO 80134
888/OP-BOOKS
www.outskirtspress.com
info@outskirtspress.com

Copyright © 2007 by Patrick O'Connor

www.collegeisyours.com
collegeisyours@comcast.net

Cover and interior design: Bonnie Schemm

Cover photo ©iStockPhoto.com. All rights reserved. Used with permission.

The opinions expressed in this manuscript are solely the opinions of the author and do not represent the opinions or thoughts of the publisher. The author has represented and warranted full ownership and/or legal right to publish all the materials in this book.

V1.0 R1.0

This book may not be reproduced, transmitted, or stored in whole or in part by any means, including graphic, electronic, or mechanical without the express written consent of the publisher except in the case of brief quotations embodied in critical articles and reviews.

Outskirts Press, Inc.
http://www.outskirtspress.com

ISBN: 978-1-4327-0574-9

Outskirts Press and the "OP" logo are trademarks belonging to Outskirts Press, Inc.

PRINTED IN THE UNITED STATES OF AMERICA

Dedication

When Ila Donnelly met Richard O'Connor, she knew he was the man she was going to marry. Dad sensed this and tried to put Mom off diplomatically, until finally he had to say he didn't think it was the right idea just yet, since she was only 14, and he had just gotten a driver's license.

In 1947 Dad finally gave in, and he and Mom married and raised three sons — Joe, who saw life as a never-ending series of intense opportunities; Brian, who is the real writer in the family, and me. Mom and Dad never went to college, but when the time came for their children to go, they saw to it we went and made the most of the experience. The only time I really remember my father being angry was when I told him I wanted to get a job while I was in college. "You have a job," he said between clenched teeth, "and that is to study." Enough said.

This book wouldn't have been possible without the kindness and wisdom of my dear wife Dianne, our fine children, dozens of friends and hundreds of colleagues, all of whom have been supportive and gracious enough to give of their hearts, hands and talents when there was absolutely nothing for them to gain in their giving, and without the patience and faith of the parents and students I have done my best to serve.

I will be grateful to them forever, in part because they understand that before the friends and colleagues, before the parents and students, and even before my own family, there were parents whose vision and vitality led me to value all there is to see, and to consider all there is that could be seen.

Mom and Dad, this book is dedicated to you.

Acknowledgments

Front cover photograph of Roeper's Hill House by Lawrence Trinkaus
Design and layout by Bonnie Schemm

Thanks to ...
Lori Lutz for reading the first draft
Gregg Goldberg for help with Chapter 3
Randall Dunn for giving me the green light
Mom for editing
Brian for the publishing counsel
Titus at Grace Publishing
Jennifer at Outskirts Press
Collin Ganio for the Latin,
J.T. Allen and the MyFootpath gang
and to Jan King, my high school counselor

SAT is a registered trademark of the College Entrance Examination Board.
AP is a registered trademark of the College Entrance Examination Board.
PSAT/NMSQT is a registered trademark of the College Entrance Examination Board and the National Merit Scholarship Corporation.
ACT is a registered trademark of the American College Testing Board, Inc.
PLAN is a registered trademark of the American College Testing Board, Inc.
Oscar is a registered trademark of the Academy of Motion Picture Arts and Sciences.
Super Bowl is a registered trademark of the National Football League.
JEOPARDY! is a registered trademark of Jeopardy! Productions, Inc.
Windows is a registered trademark of Microsoft Corporation.
in the United States and other countries.

The *Princeton Review*, Review.com and Counselo-U-Matic
are trademarks of Princeton Review, Inc. and its affiliates.

Neither the College Entrance Examination Board, the National Merit Scholarship Corporation, Princeton Review, Inc., the American College Testing Board, Inc.,
the Academy of Motion Picture Arts and Sciences, the National Football League,
Jeopardy! Productions, Inc., nor Microsoft Corporation
had anything to do with the creation or publication of this book, nor have they endorsed it.

Table of Contents

	WELCOME	2
	INTRODUCTION	4
1.	THE BIG PICTURE AND THE MIDDLE ROAD	6
2.	THE KEY TO SUCCESS	8
3.	THE TWO KINDS OF GENUINE COMMUNITY SERVICE	10
4.	EXTRACURRICULAR ACTIVITIES	12
5.	MORE THAN A CHECKLIST	14
6.	TESTS TO TAKE IN 10TH GRADE	16
7.	THE BASICS OF VISITING A COLLEGE	18
8.	HIGHLY SELECTIVE COLLEGES	20
9	TALKING WITH YOUR PARENTS ABOUT COLLEGE	22
10.	WORKING WITH YOUR COUNSELOR	24
11.	COLLEGE FAIRS	26
12.	MORE SEARCH TOOLS	28
13.	ACT AND SAT	30
14.	TEST PREP	32
15.	SENIOR SCHEDULE AND MORE ON COLLEGE VISITS	34
16.	MAKING THE LIST	36
17.	SAFETY SCHOOLS AND TRANSFERRING	38
18.	COMMUNITY COLLEGES AND GRADE POINT AVERAGES	40
19.	APPLICATION DEADLINES	42
20.	COLLEGE COSTS	44
21.	LETTERS OF RECOMMENDATION — THE BIG PICTURE	46
22	LETTERS — THE NUTS AND BOLTS	48
23.	LINING UP AN INTERVIEW	50
24.	SHOWTIME	52
25.	ESSAYS	54
26.	THE FINAL CHECK	56
27.	THREE KINDS OF DECISIONS	58
28.	WAITLISTS	60
29.	GENESIS	62
30	FOR SOMEDAY (I HOPE NOT)	64
31.	WHAT'S NEXT?	66
32.	600 WORDS FOR PARENTS	69
	ABOUT THE ROEPER SCHOOL	71
	ABOUT NACAC	72
	ABOUT THE AUTHOR	73

Welcome

For most students, choosing a college starts with a book. The book is usually large, heavy and a little intimidating in appearance. To most people, this makes sense — since picking a college is a big, weighty decision, you need a big, weighty book.

The truth is, choosing a college shouldn't start with a book — it should start with your heart. After 12 years in the learning business, you should have some ideas about yourself — who you are, what you like, the kinds of places you like to visit, the kinds of people you like to be with. By building your college choices on what you like, you're making sure that every college you put on your list (and at the start, there can be as many as 20) has enough of the things you like to make it an OK place to study and to live. That last part can't be emphasized enough; this isn't just a place where you sit in a classroom and go home at three o'clock. This is your new home as well, even if you're not going to live on campus.

A few additional rules here. First, you don't have to know what you're going to major in before you pick a college. Yes, if music is a real passion, you'd be wise to apply to colleges that offer music — but most students pick a major that's offered by many colleges, and most students will change their majors at least twice in college. So majors can help, but if you don't have one, don't panic.

Second, you don't have to know what you're going to do with the rest of your life before you pick a college. This is **really** important because, while your friends will be cool with this, your parents, your girlfriend/boyfriend's parents, your neighbors and your Aunt Henrietta may not be (see *Chapter 16*). Being able to pay your own light bill matters, so it does deserve some thought — but the hot jobs when college is over probably don't even exist now. If you have an idea, a dream, or the results of a career test, plug them into the college equation — but it's not the only part of the solution, and if it doesn't exist, it doesn't need to be a part at all right now.

Third, if you find you don't really know that much about yourself, don't open the book — every college will look good to you. Instead, try asking yourself these five questions:

1. What three things about my high school would I like to see at my college?

2. What three things about my high school do I never want to see again?

3. What three classes, clubs or programs should my high school offer that it doesn't offer now?

4. What parts of my home town do I like and — well — not like?

5. What three things would I like to do that I've never done before?

This isn't a comprehensive set of questions — just five to get you going. Once you have those questions answered, you're ready to open the book or go online and do a college search. Size of school, location of school, campus life, major — you're ready to take on most of those questions now. And don't worry about cost just yet — we'll take that on in due time. For now, lead with your heart, your brain and a little, weighty book.

Enjoy.

Introduction

College admissions offices aren't perfect. Every year, students get admitted who end up dropping out, never coming, or getting grades that put them on the "Dean's List" nobody likes to talk about. On top of that, students get denied by colleges where they would have been great students, active leaders, and wealthy alumni donors. Either way, colleges hate to make mistakes, and they do the best they can — but the system isn't perfect.

Take admissions essays. Many colleges don't require essays; these colleges rely heavily on how you did on one test you took in your junior year of high school, which, to me, is just begging for trouble — but more on that later. Colleges that do ask for essays usually leave the topic up to you because they want to hear about your life and what you think is important — as long as you don't use more than 500 or 600 words.

That's a bad vibe right off the jump. It seems like the colleges are convinced nothing could be so important in your life as to take up more than 500 words, and if you DARE use 501 words to talk about it — well, you're toast. It seems like they might as well say, "Tell us why you love your life, but be quick about it."

Not a perfect approach to building a meaningful relationship, right?

The thing is, there's another way to look at this. To begin with, admissions officers care about you very much. I have yet to meet a more compassionate, intelligent, thoughtful group of people.

Second, a 500-word essay doesn't always have a 500-word limit. We'll talk more about this later, but if you're telling a great story, many admissions officers would gladly read 550 words or so. I wouldn't push it much past 550, but I think you get the idea …

… Which is this: Much of what you think about getting into college isn't quite right. Admissions officers aren't robots; essay limits aren't always absolute; test scores may not matter that much; college rankings are — hey, I'd better slow down. It's hard to say where all of these myths came from, but they're doing a lot of damage to students and families; I wrote this book to help turn that around.

Just a heads up before we get started. Just like college admissions, this book isn't perfect. I've tried to give you some general advice on the most important topics in selecting a college that's right for you, but putting the right blend of ideas together for individual needs and interests in one book is impossible. That's why there's an e-mail address at the end of the book. Read one chapter a day; go away and really think about what the ideas mean to you. Once you're done with the whole book, e-mail me your questions about your individual needs, and we'll see what we can do — for free.

See? You just got yourself a personal college counselor.

Since we're in this together, I've limited my chapters to 600 words — just like some of your college essays. I'll want to say more, but I might bore some of you, and then you'd go looking for college help from the sources that made you nervous in the first place. Don't look back — you've got a future to build, and you need fresh, good information.

Ready?

P.S. *That part about the 500-word essay really being a 550-word essay? That won't work at Yale. There, if you get to 501, you really are on your way to being toast.*

Chapter 1
THE BIG PICTURE AND THE MIDDLE ROAD

Your parents will tell you applying to college was easy when they were young. According to them, they got up early one Saturday morning, took a test they'd never heard of, applied to one or two colleges their friends applied to, got in to at least one of them, and that was it. Simple.

Fast forward to today. Your friends are freaking about college, the home page of your computer is a "vocabulary question of the day" Web site, and even your parents — the ones who tell you how easy it was for them to apply to college — made you volunteer at a soup kitchen at age six, since that "looks good" to a college. With all of that going on, it's hard to believe that a college choice could be simple — after all, even the college rankings say it's hard.

To those of you who hope your choice is as easy as your parents', and to those of you who are test-prepped up to here, let me offer another choice:

Live a rich, full life today, and apply only to colleges you love.

Colleges want students who get up every day and live, who go to high schools with limited choices and blaze new trails in learning that turn teachers' heads, or go to fancy high schools and squeeze every drop of learning out of every challenging class. They want students who have seen a problem down the block and implemented a powerful solution, and they want students who flew halfway across the world and gave of their hands, hearts and minds to people they will never see again. They want students who will push the status quo and lead the culture to new journeys, and they want students who celebrate the status quo by finding ways to make it better.

In other words, they want students who know who they are, and really *do*.

To those of you who have had test prep flash cards since birth, it might be time to retool a little. Colleges don't want students who just do the right things and say the right things and get the right scores. Sure, they take those kinds of students all the time, but they don't want to. Colleges will take students who let their lights shine and know themselves any day, except the real doers are few and far between — and if you think they can't tell the difference, you are vastly underestimating the intelligence of these folks.

At the same time, those of you who are hoping college selection will be a cakewalk need to ramp it up a gear or two. It could be the college you're dreaming of is just the place for you, but if the best reason you can give for going to that school is, "Why not?," it's time you introduced yourself to your passion and purpose for learning. It not only makes each day a little brighter, it improves your chances of finishing college once you start.

It would be easy to believe that the key to college is training; that would give you a reason to be so busy with so much essay coaching and such that you wouldn't have time to think about what you're doing. It would also be easy to believe that your dream school would meet your needs — unless you haven't been awake enough to know what your needs really are. Like most of life, there's a better middle road to take if your destination is college — and your navigation system starts on the next page.

Chapter 2
THE KEY TO SUCCESS

Ninth graders are either reading this book because they're overly jonesed about college or because they can't leave the house until they finish. Read the next four chapters, then tell the folks I said to come back next year.

The most important thing every college cares about is grades. Unless we're talking art or music school, your admission to a college most depends on getting great grades in challenging classes — not just in 11th grade, not once you're in college, but starting now. Not everyone can do this all of the time — in fact, very few people can — but the closer you get to this level, the more choices you have, and the college selection process is all about having choices.

So how do you get good grades? Be a good student.

I know, I know — that's *some* counseling, right? But most people don't go through high school as students — they go as guests, waiting for the teachers to tell them to do something. Once asked, they do homework, pass tests, write papers, get OK grades — but they never put their hearts into it, or really think about what they're doing. No wonder students are a wreck when they fill out college applications; they've spent three years doing things that never really made sense to them, and when colleges ask them to write about the most important things they've learned as a student, they don't know what to say.

It's time to stop the stress and the guessing, even though your friends may be college bound, thanks to that terrible twosome. If your math teacher assigns 15 problems, do those, and the next three problems after that; then read the math book (yeah — **read** the math book) to make sure what you learned today makes sense with what you learned yesterday. If your English teacher assigns 15 pages of reading, take notes on the reading as you go; this will require reading, stopping, thinking and writing, and you can already do all of those things. Add to these notes every night, and imagine the teacher's surprise next week when someone actually answers the question, "How does all of this tie together?"

If these last two ideas scare you, you might want to sit down. When your history teacher asks for a 250-word paper, write 400 or 500 — in your own words — after you've compared the information in your textbook with what you learned from two credible history Web sites (and as you write, don't forget that "reading, stopping, thinking and writing" thing). When you type the essay, put the words *"ROUGH DRAFT"* in big letters on the top page. Three days before the paper's due, ask your teacher to look it over with you before school; take notes during your meeting, and use those when you write the final draft, which is turned in on time.

These three things alone might not improve your grades, but you get the idea. Colleges like students who care about learning and who are good at learning; if you push yourself and go the extra mile, you'll soon be better at both (even if you're currently getting As just on natural ability). This might require some changes in your social schedule (*hey, there's always study groups!*), and you may have to speak with a teacher or two about study skills techniques, but two or three months from now, you'll thank me — as a real student and as a serious candidate for college.

Chapter 3
THE TWO KINDS OF GENUINE COMMUNITY SERVICE

Good students give more to their studies, and good people make a better world. Colleges (and the rest of us) like to see both.

So here's Key Number 2 — go out now and be the good person you are, demonstrating that through community service and extracurricular activities.

Generally, there are two kinds of community service. The first is a regular, dedicated, volunteer effort to improve the conditions of your community that has no direct impact on your own life — in other words, you're making things better for others more than you are for yourself. This would include things like volunteering at a soup kitchen, school, retirement home, tutoring program, a place of worship, the Red Cross — you get the idea. Volunteer work at a business would not count — that's more like an internship, externship or job shadowing — which is important (see *Chapter 4*), but it isn't community service. Similarly, chores around your house don't count — they are also important, but that's more like, well, life.

"Required" volunteer work — community service or volunteer work you *HAD* to do to fulfill some kind of requirement (graduation requirement, Boy Scouts, being allowed to still live at home) is a little different, and a little confusing — you volunteered to do it because you had to? Still, it's improving the community, so it counts — but in fairness to the colleges you're applying to, you need to note that you completed this work as part of a requirement.

Regular, dedicated work means you're giving consistently. This generally means one to two hours a week, or for an intense period of time during the summer — starting in 9th grade. Remember, you're doing this because you want the world to be better and are willing to do something about it; the wise people who review college applications can tell if you're doing this just to suck up to them, and that's very unflattering for everyone involved. If you're having trouble genuinely wanting to make a difference, go read the essays by Isabel Allende and Miles Goodwin in *This I Believe*, then come back when you're focused.

The second kind of community service is just as important, but less frequent. This is "roll up your sleeves" community service, where a brief and/or urgent need requires a concentrated period of time. Examples here include helping your local school put up new playground equipment for a day, boxing canned goods for a few hours at church to send to hurricane victims, spending a spring break with Habitat for Humanity, shoveling driveways of neighbors for free after the big snow, and welcoming students at school orientation in the fall. Individually, these efforts are important, but small; combined, they are important and mighty. Colleges love to see this kind of community service, since it shows you are willing to pitch in on a moment's notice and make a difference — and we all know the power of small acts of kindness in both the lives of those you serve and in those who do the service.

In either case, community service only truly works if you are doing it out of a sense of love — for a neighbor, a stranger, or the world. College admissions officers have a way of peering into your heart that might be considered a little scary, except that it's good for us. It makes us keep the bigger picture in mind, that life isn't about glory or recognition — it's about living a rich, full life.

P.S. *If one of those two essays doesn't make you cry, you can't go to college. Sorry. I forbid it.*

Chapter 4
EXTRACURRICULAR ACTIVITIES

Just like community service, extracurricular activities are important — but keep these key points in mind:

- Extracurriculars can be thought of as hobbies or interests — sports, clubs, summer classes, travel, work, and internships are the big ones.

- You want a mix of extracurriculars. It's OK to play sports for four years, or have the same job for a long time — but don't let one or two things be the only things on your list for all of high school. You're shooting for consistency **and** variety.

- Not all extracurriculars exist at school. Since there are lots of activities offered at schools that you can't find in other places, you should try some of them — but look around your local community center, library, YMCA, or Boys and Girls' Club, too.

- Extracurriculars and community service are two different things, but they can overlap. If your high school basketball team runs the elementary basketball league in the summer, you're doing both; the same with the French Club that visits retirement centers on a regular basis. If you see a chance to mix the two, use your creative leadership skills — it makes for a great life and a unique item for a college app.

- It's more than OK to start a new club in your school or community. Filling a need also shows creativity and leadership — just do your best to include others, and create a solid foundation for the club to grow on **after** you're gone. (*Selflessness rules in choosing a college!*)

- Work hard, but keep balanced. If you're doing too much at once, your grades go down, you lose your focus, and nothing seems fun. If your team demands all of your time, back off on community service for a few months; if it's crunch time at work, you might have to pass up the Spanish Club this semester. There'll be enough time, provided you use enough wisdom to balance your studies, your community service, and your extracurriculars.

- Keep a log of all of the extracurricular activities as you try them. Waiting until senior year isn't the way to go — 9th grade will be hazy by then, and you want a clear list. Use a notebook (don't use a computer, because you might be using a different one come 12th grade), and have your parents and friends review the list, since they'll remember things you'll forget.

- Give yourself some credit. Your summer trip to Mexico each year may be a family reunion to you, but it's travel to a different country and culture to a college. And what if your reunion is in Georgia instead? It still puts you in a different place — put it down!

- At the same time, be clear and fair. There is a limit to making yourself sound good, and the limit is honesty. Detroit is about 10 minutes away from Canada, so my students sometimes tell colleges they are "international travelers." That's no way to build a relationship with a college. If you went to Canada, tell them that.

- Leave a page in your notebook for any awards or recognitions you may receive for anything — school, community service, or extracurriculars. Colleges care about these, too, and they'll be easy to find if it's just a page away from your activities.

Your diet of extracurriculars should be like food at a good Super Bowl® party — a great main course or two and interesting smaller appetizers. Do that, and you'll be ready for college, life and some awesome tailgate parties.

Chapter 5
MORE THAN A CHECKLIST

Since many colleges ask for lists — what sports you do, what clubs you've joined, what work you do in your community — some student develop a "checklist attitude" towards community service and extracurriculars. Instead of doing these things because they're great things to do, students see them as one more "thing," one more task to knock off to get into a great college. Then, just like 9th grade gym, once you're in, you're finished with that for good.

The truth is, it doesn't work that way. First, colleges can sort out the truly committed from the "list completers" in a heartbeat. The folks who are looking to beef up a college application join a dozen groups junior year, and give two hours total to each; the givers are active in a group or two starting in (or even before) 9th grade, contributing two to five hours a week to helping those in need, something they believe in. This kind of commitment usually leads to leadership opportunities or chances to take a volunteer group in a new direction — but even if it doesn't, colleges will notice when a student gave 300 – 700 hours to a cause during high school and still had time for studies, families and a couple of extracurriculars.

Second, just like good study habits, these things improve your learning in a big way. Giving up your TV time or chat room time for the swim team, the chess club, and the homeless shelter puts you in the center of the real world, where you learn about the give and take of life, the differences between people, and the importance of everyone pitching in and doing their best. Colleges have a name for that kind of learning — they call it wisdom — and it is a highly-valued commodity. By giving to the world outside of the classroom, you are showing an interest in the world and a willingness to challenge yourself — what college wouldn't love to see that?

Third, doing these things now gets you ready for — hang on here — life after college. I know that's a few years and a zillion Friday nights down the road, but it's coming, and you need to be ready. If you can practice juggling school, service and fun now, you'll be a Zen master at it by 25, and you'll stay with it until you're 125. Imagine a world where everybody knows how to work hard, give back and let go. That would be like — like college forever!

It's usually right here where students say, "

> **Yeah, but I stink at everything."**

Look — go to your town's health club this Saturday morning. The place won't be filled with athletic superstars, but with people who love to work out. Some will be ripped; some will be wearing trendy outfits; and some will be struggling to bench press 80 pounds — but they'll all be doing the best they can, trying to make a difference with what they've got and loving the challenge they've made for themselves.

And that's the whole idea — love what you do so much that what the guy next to you thinks about you becomes irrelevant. Find a cause or two and some extracurriculars that mean something to you, and give your all. You might not get an award or a team captainship to throw on a college application — but then again, you might. Either way, you'll have four solid years of taking a stand, of giving, living, and learning beyond the world of books — and that can make a huge difference, both to a college and to the world.

Chapter 6
TESTS TO TAKE IN 10TH GRADE

If there are any 9th graders here, let me gently recommend you put this book down and sign up for remedial math — you've had your four chapters, so your work here is finished for now.

In order to make a great college selection, 10th graders need to do four things. First, keep doing everything you started in 9th grade. Strong grades in challenging classes, frequent community service and some solid extracurricular activities are the foundation of the House of College Knowledge, so keep cementing away at that foundation. (*Get it — Foundation? House? Cement? Boy — tough crowd!*)

Second, it's time to build some windows in that house, and the first two involve four-letter words. (*Oh, sure — now I have your attention.*)

The PSAT® gives juniors a peek at how the SAT® works. Let me say that again — it's designed to give **juniors** a chance to see how the SAT works. The scores juniors earn on the PSAT may qualify them for scholarships through the National Merit Corporation®. About 15 years ago, some 10th graders thought it might be a good idea to take the PSAT as sophomores — that way, they could get a feel for the test, then smoke it as juniors and grab some cash. This idea soon made sense to a lot of 10th graders, so now many schools offer the PSAT to 10th graders.

It's OK to take the PSAT in 10th grade, as long as you'll be OK with getting a less than perfect score. The PSAT measures Verbal Reasoning, Math and Writing, based on what the test writers think juniors should know — and you're a sophomore. Since there's a decent chance you haven't had everything that's on the test (and that's **really** true if you're not taking Geometry or Algebra 2), your scores might not be what you think they should be. If you're cool with that, and you want to jump in and see what these tests are all about, go for it; if you think your chances at an Ivy League school will be trashed because your 10th grade PSAT could be low, let it go …

… Or try this. Your high school gets practice versions of the PSAT — if you're taking the test, you'll get a copy when you sign up for the test (use it to get ready!). If you're not taking the test, wait until the PSAT has been given, then ask your counselor for any leftover practice tests. Take it home, time yourself, then check your answers. It's free, it's simple to do, and nobody gets hurt.

Whether you do PSAT or not, 10th graders should take the PLAN®. PLAN is a preliminary ACT®, and ACT is the other test many colleges use as part of the admission process. PLAN is designed to be given in 10th grade, so the results you get will give you an honest picture of how well you know the stuff you've been studying. Finally, if tests just take too much out of you, you may qualify for extra time or other accommodations to take PLAN or PSAT — ask your school now.

Some people spaz about tests, because they see them as windows into their minds or souls. Taking PLAN and PSAT as 10th graders is really a one-way window, since you get to peek at what colleges expect you to know, but colleges will never ask to see your scores. This is too good to pass up — make your move!

Chapter 7
THE BASICS OF VISITING A COLLEGE

High school athletes watch the pros to get tips and get inspired. High school artists visit museums to see classic art, so they can create new art. High school writers read the works that made new inroads, so they are juiced to forge new paths.

And that's why 10th graders visit college campuses.

Hanging out on a college campus can give you a natural buzz, a sense that something's going on here, that maybe this place can help you make some dreams come true. That's where you want to be — that's the attitude that will get you into a college that's right for you and help you make sense out of high school.

So the third thing you do as a 10th grader is take a road trip (with your parents, if possible).

There are lots of ways to visit a college, but here are some ideas:

- Start local. You can learn a lot by visiting any college campus, even if you're not sure you'd really go there. With any luck, the first thing you'll learn is that every college has lots of fast food places, 24-hour stores, and cool places to buy sweatshirts. Beyond that, you need to figure out what makes a college special to you — a particular major, class size, the way the profs treat the students — and the college across the street can help you sort some of that out as well as a college across the country.

- Take a tour, and fill out the registration card (this is important — trust me). College admissions offices usually host campus tours — call them two weeks ahead of time and sign up. Remember, the tour is their chance to show what they think are the best parts of the college — and that can say a lot. If a tour guide doesn't really answer your questions (ask a lot), or if you get the feeling the college isn't very interesting, this might not be the place for you.

- Customize your visit. When you call about the tour, ask to sit in on classes (that's right — you DON'T visit a college on a day when there are no classes), or to talk with a prof in the department you're interested in. If you care about something special — the workout areas, the research labs, the library — ask to see it. Ask to see a dorm. Some colleges won't show them to you, but ask anyway. Try the food if you'd like, but if your parents are going along, I'd hit them up for a meal out instead. Of course, you can also go to the big game or concert that's on campus — just be sure to see some classes in action.

- Compare colleges. As you visit each college, write down your impressions right after the visit is over. This may seem a little geeky, but since you'll be visiting lots of campuses over a few years, it's the best way to remember what you saw and to sort out colleges you like from those you don't.

If you do a campus visit the right way, you'll learn a lot about college — and even more about yourself. Both of these things can inspire the learning you're doing in high school and the life you're living right now. We have a name for that in college counseling — it's called a deal. Take it.

P.S. *Whether you get to a campus or not, read* Colleges That Change Lives *by Lauren Pope. It's not quite a campus visit, but it will point you in the right direction about the purpose of college.*

Chapter 8

HIGHLY-SELECTIVE COLLEGES

With some college visits behind you and the wisdom of Lauren Pope in you (I'm telling you, read that book), you might be thinking serious college thoughts. You know who you are; you know what you want; you're past what others think about you; and you've learned how to work hard.

Maybe it's time to think about a highly-selective college.

First, an explanation. A highly-selective college (at least my definition) is a college that admits about 15% or less of everyone who applies there. The number of these colleges has gone up, and their admit rates have gone down — some to as low as 8%. For confused folks, these numbers lead them to apply ("I might be one of the lucky 11%!"), or not apply ("Man, nobody applies there anymore — it's too crowded!"). In either case, it shouldn't be about the numbers; it should be about whether the college matches up with you. If it doesn't, who cares if you get into a school that's not for you? But if it does …

… Well, it's decision time. Truth is, most students don't get into these colleges because of luck — it's because they saw what they wanted and went the many extra miles to get there. For example, a couple of these colleges ask if you've done any published research in high school. We're not talking a lab report or a winning science fair project; we're talking worked with a college professor on a new aspect of an old idea, and contributed enough that your name is in a respected scholarly journal somewhere.

At seventeen.

National champion debaters, the best cellist in the Eastern US, champion figure skaters, the winner of the World Math Decathlon — if their academic credentials are OK, where do you think they stand with other A students? That's not to say As aren't important; but when everyone who applies to a college has As, you can't blame the college for saying, as nicely but as clearly as possible, "Great. Do you have anything else?" And don't think you can escape by saying, "But I went to a great high school," since they'll tell you everyone else did, too — and they did.

If you think this can be devastating, you're right — that's why I'm mentioning it now. If you want to keep the option of a highly selective college open, you're wise to start pursuing your interests in ways others do not. This isn't about padding a college application with things that mean nothing to you; this is about enriching your life with something that means a great deal to you and showing that care to the world at an amazing level. The hours of practice, the TV given up for summer programs, the time away from family — this is a demonstrated passion that's way more than giving up Saturday mornings for test prep. This is yet another version of living a rich, full life, about a level of commitment and achievement you just can't bluff.

It's certainly true that selective colleges take a lot of straight-A students who weren't the ambassador to Spain at age 12, but if you look closely, you'll see way more students there who have sent the message that they know who they are, and who they are is seriously committed. No one will judge you if you shoot for this target and miss, or decide not to aim for it at all. The heads-up here is so you know what's expected if a highly-selective college is calling to you, and so you won't judge yourself this way, either.

Chapter 9
TALKING WITH YOUR PARENTS ABOUT COLLEGE

It's usually right about here that I catch it.

> *"Take my parents with me to visit colleges?*
> *Dude, why don't you just tell me to take them to homecoming, too?"*

I hear you — but here's the thing. As soon as you start taking tests and visiting colleges, most parents freak — they shouldn't (neither should you), but they do. It's like I said back in Chapter 2 — even though your parents will tell you college applications were a breeze for them, the minute it's about you, that cute pudgy baby in the widdle blanket, even the most laid back parent can start scoping the Internet for deals on test prep computer programs. In fairness, it's not always this way, but when it happens, it ain't fun, since now you have not only your college issues to deal with, you've got theirs, too.

It's time to hold hands and cross the street together.

In addition to being a college counselor, I teach American Government, and one of the interesting things about government is that both sides can be right at the same time. It's the same thing with college; you want some space to sort things out, get (and keep) your head clear, and check out some schools. Cool. Your parents want you to have a good future, make sure you're safe, and be sure they aren't throwing college tuition away at some school where students go to more football games than classes. Fair enough.

The way you both get what you want is the weekly meeting. At the beginning of the college selection process, student and parents agree to meet once a week for 20 minutes to talk about college. During this 20 minutes, it's OK to ask about anything related to college. Your parents can ask if you're taking enough college prep classes, if any colleges are coming to visit your high school, if there is an application deadline coming up, if you made that appointment with your counselor — anything. At the same time, you can ask about anything, too — why you have to apply to the college they went to, how they would feel if you took a year off before starting college, why they embarrassed you by asking that lame question at the last college tour — anything. Nobody loses their cool; nobody interrupts; and everybody ends the meeting with a written list of what they need to find out to answer someone else's questions. Unless the answers are time sensitive, the answers are shared at the next meeting.

There's no hard and fast rule about when to start these meetings. Some parents need to start them once the practice PLAN comes home, while others will stay calm until Labor Day of senior year — but if you want to score some major points, make sure you're the one who suggests the idea of starting weekly meetings. This will give your parents the correct impression that you've got your act together, and that you care about what they have to say. It will also give you a little more breathing room — once parents know you've got things under control, they're less inclined to clip your wings and more inclined to let you fly.

I've seen a lot of students make great college plans on their own, but having the folks along to root you on is like summer baseball — it's more fun to hit the ball knowing someone will cheer when you go yard. The weekly meeting will do that for you.

P.S. *When you suggest the meetings, make sure they involve food — that they pay for.*

Chapter 10
WORKING WITH YOUR COUNSELOR

In case you thought you were out of the woods, your parents aren't the only adults you have to help stay organized. Another one is your college counselor.

Go ahead. I'll wait.

> *"Dog, not only do I have my own mess to keep straight, but now I have to put my parents and my counselor on my back? I don't even know who my counselor is, and they sure don't know me."*

Right — and that's the problem. If you look at most college applications, there's a part your counselor has to fill out about the classes you've taken, your grades and your class rank. There's also a spot where your counselor can make comments about you — the space may be small, but it's still there. One of three things will happen with this space: It stays blank; your counselor scribbles something in it that could describe anybody; your counselor has so many helpful things to say about you, they have to write, "continued on attached sheet."

Two questions here. First, if you gave your counselor that form today, which option would they choose? Second, which one are you rooting for?

Sounds like you have work to do.

This isn't hard. For the first two years of high school, see your counselor when you need to — to change a schedule, discuss a personal problem, apply for a summer program — and, if they have time, talk about college. Like it or not, your counselor is way over-worked — schedule changes, college counseling, career plans and personal guidance for 500 students keeps them busy — so the great group-counseling programs they run and an occasional "check-in" from you will go a long way in meeting both of your needs. So, go if you need to; if not, space is cool.

The time to ramp things up is February of junior year. If your school is like most, your counselor will see you in March to put your senior schedule together. By the end of February (*right — February*), you want to type up your community service work and extracurricular activities from your notebook (*remember your notebook?*) along with awards and recognitions you've received. You also want to have your senior year schedule together before you have your scheduling meeting — *read that again* — and you want to put everything in an inexpensive pocket folder that has your name on it.

I hope you see where this is going. When it's time for your scheduling meeting, you hand over the folder and start talking first:

> *Hi, Mrs. Jones. I know you're really busy, so I got a copy of my transcript from your secretary and planned out my schedule already. I also wanted you to know I'm registering for the April SAT and ACT, and I'm visiting three colleges over spring break. I don't know if I'll see you before it's time to apply for colleges, so I've enclosed a list of my extracurriculars and community service projects, and I've highlighted the ones I'm most proud of. I've also put my cellphone number at the top of the page so you can call me when you're filling out my applications if you have any questions. Thanks for helping me with this — if I have any questions, what's the best way to contact you?"*

I promise you — if you do this, your counselor will remember you and look for excuses to see you from now on.

Counselor on track; counselor off back.

Nice work, dog.

COLLEGE FAIRS

Having that conversation with your counselor at the end of 11th grade requires some serious prep time throughout the rest of 11th grade. There are four things you'll do junior year to make a good college choice, and the most important one is to visit more colleges. From Chapter 7, you know the basics of campus visits. As a junior, you'll need to look a little closer, a little longer, and a little harder …

… But before you hit the campuses, you should do some homework at a local college fair. College visits cost time and money, and you'll need to make the most of both junior year. College fairs help you do that — held in fall and spring, a fair can have representatives from up to 400 colleges, all eager to talk to you about their college and your life. Many fairs feature information on choosing and applying to college and financial aid, and most fairs are free.

With so many colleges at a fair, it's easy to get intimidated — so plan ahead. Take a pen, a highlighter, an unofficial copy of your transcript, and five questions **committed to memory** that will help you learn more about a college. What you ask is up to you — majors, food, chances for research, cost, social life — just make sure the answers will help you decide if this place is worth a closer look.

At the fair, get a map of where the booths of the colleges are located. BEFORE you go onto the floor, highlight the colleges you're interested in. (This same list might be on a Web site — even better, since you can research colleges ahead of time.) Once you're at a booth, you might have to wait to ask questions — this is good! Use this time to listen to what the representative is saying to other students — since they will most likely be discussing general questions, you can use your time to ask more detailed stuff.

Once it's your turn, get busy. "Hi, my name is (NO student does this, but you should; it shows confidence, and gives the rep the chance to remember you), and I go to Captain Jack High School." From here, you want to ask your questions; make eye contact as they answer, and don't rush them.

If you feel you're hitting a good vibe, pull out your transcript and say, "Just one more question. I'm putting my senior schedule together. Here's what I've taken so far; what other courses would your college like to see me take?" ABSOLUTELY, POSITIVELY NOBODY does this at a college fair, which is why you should. Most of the time, you'll actually get some great advice (or even a scholarship offer), but don't be surprised if they don't know what to say — either way, you'll be remembered by reps in a very positive way. Thank them for their time, fill out a registration card (that's important), tell them you hope they come by your school to visit, and move on.

Make quick notes on this college **before** you visit the next booth. You can use your "waiting time" at the next booth to do this, but write at least something down — you don't want to confuse your colleges.

If you can do about seven to 10 colleges and spend time at an information session of interest to you, call it a victory with an after-fair pizza. (This is why you bring your parents along — to pay!) You now have some solid information on which colleges are road-trip worthy, and some solid information about yourself as well — truly a dynamic duo.

MORE SEARCH TOOLS

There are other great ways to scope out college possibilities without leaving home. Most of them are easy; all of them are helpful; and one popular one should be avoided — read on.

A great way to find out more about a college is to let the college come to you. Many colleges send admission representatives to your high school in the fall to tell you about their college. A list of these colleges is posted in the counseling center or the main office; every Thursday, write down the colleges that will be coming next week, look them up in your college guide (more on that soon), then get a pass from counseling to visit with the rep. In some high schools, reps are only allowed to come before or after school or during lunch, and some will only let reps talk to students during lunch in the lunchroom. (*Whoa — talk about leaving an impression!*) If your school has these rules, give up the free time and go anyway — not many students will do this, which is (*everybody sing along now*) exactly why you should.

The same goes for hotel visits. Sometimes reps have such tight schedules they can only hold visits for lots of students at a hotel ballroom, in the evening or on weekends. The same rules apply here — do your homework, and go if it sounds good, bringing along your compadres and family for fun, along with dinner before or ice cream after. Whether it's in a hotel or the school's lunchroom, take along your college fair questions; fill out a card (even if you've talked to this rep or visited the campus before); introduce yourself to the rep (*nothing like face time*); ask a great question, and write down what you think once you're home.

If at any point you're not sure you're heading in the right direction, a college search might be helpful. ***Collegeboard.com*** ® lets you sort out colleges a million ways, from majors to location to activities to you name it. ***Princetonreview.com*** ® has the Counselor-O-Matic®, which asks you questions to point you in the right direction. These sites and others can give you some general direction and lots of schools to consider.

Another great source is college guides — books or magazines that describe colleges and what they have to offer. Guides give you a solid look at all parts of a college. A good guide will tell you about classes, the campus, social life, and atmosphere, and a great guide will include interviews with students, who will give you the straight scoop. There are a lot of these around — try your counseling office or local public library ...

... But while you're there, avoid books or magazines with college rankings. College rankings are designed to tell you what the "best" colleges are, based on the opinion of someone who doesn't even know what you're looking for. Unfortunately, well-meaning parents love this stuff, especially if the rankings include the opinions of university presidents. Now, university presidents are nice people, but how many of them have you split a pizza with this week? You don't need to read a magazine to find out Southwestern Michigan State is a great college; you need to find out if SMS is a great college for *you*. College guides will help you with that, and college rankings won't — so save your time and money, and skip the rankings.

Chapter 13
ACT AND SAT

As you're scoping out college visits, you'll have to set aside a couple of Saturday mornings for college testing. I know you'd rather spend Saturday morning in fuzzy pajama bottoms and a T-shirt your parents won't let you wear to school, but sometimes we make sacrifices in the name of higher education, and this is one of those times.

The testing ground rules should be familiar. You know what the SAT looks like from your PSAT testing; ditto for the ACT and your PLAN testing. One big difference is that the SAT and ACT contain writing sections, where you have to write an actual essay on a topic they give you, at the test site, in about 25 minutes. The writing test is optional on ACT, but take it — you don't want to find the school of your dreams this summer, only to discover they require the ACT writing test you didn't take this spring.

If you're trying to figure out which test to take, that's easy — take both in February or April of junior year. It's likely you'll score much better on one test than the other, but your PSAT and PLAN scores don't really predict which test that will be. Once you know which one you can groove on, you might want to take it again in June of your junior year, just to make sure you've done your best. You don't have to worry which test is required by the colleges of your dreams; every four-year college that recruits nationally will take either the ACT or the SAT — so figure out the one that's best for you, and work from your strength.

Registration for both tests is best done online, at ***www.collegeboard.com*** (SAT) and ***www.act.org*** (ACT). Sample test questions are online too; if you need more, bookstores sell additional samples. The real tests aren't cheap, but they cost a whole lot more if you miss a deadline and register late — so pay attention now, or pay serious cash later. (A limited number of fee waivers are also available for these tests — see your counseling office.) Since April is a big test date, register for April early in your junior year. Not every high school gives the tests, and if all the test sites close to you are full, you may have to drive a while (like, to a different state!) to take them. If you want to qualify for extra time or accommodations, start very early.

In addition to ACT and SAT, there is yet another breed of test — the SAT Subject Tests. Unlike the SAT (aka, the SAT Reasoning Test), these tests are only an hour long and measure your understanding of a specific subject — things like Biology, Math, and Foreign Language. Some colleges want you to take two or three of these tests in addition to taking the ACT or the Reasoning SAT. Most of these colleges will let you decide which Subject Tests to take, but some will require specific ones (like Math, if you're an Engineering Major). Since the requirements vary from school to school and year to year, check the college's Web site to get their requirements — then check again in August before senior year to make sure they haven't changed.

You sign up for these tests at the same Web site as SAT, and since the tests are only one hour long, you can take up to three tests on the same Saturday morning — leaving more time for *jammieology*, which, regrettably, is not a college major — at least not an official one, anyway.

Chapter 14
TEST PREP

Registering for the tests is easy — the harder part is getting ready for them. There are a zillion options here, including a couple I bet you haven't thought of. Here we go:

- **_Timing_** SAT and ACT are designed to measure what students know in the spring of the junior year. Some students take these tests earlier than spring, but I'd be careful — you might not know all of the math or English on the tests if you take them sooner. Also, remember that you can take the tests in fall of your senior year, if necessary, through December.

    With SAT Subject Tests, the timing may be different. Most students take these as seniors, in October or December — it spreads the testing out — but if you're not taking a Biology class when you're taking the Biology test, you may be rusty. Using a test prep booklet solves this, so long as you have the discipline to use it — if not, take the test at the end of the class.

- **_Re-testing_** Some people get ready for a test by taking it over and over … and over! Scores do tend to go up in the second testing, but not much after that, unless you study. So seven times is out, unless you need a specific score to nail a scholarship.

- **_Self-help_** Between the sample tests, test prep booklets, Web sites, and computer programs, there are all kinds of ways to study at your own pace — but will you? It's easy enough to say you'll study on Saturday or after homework's done; most students need a parental assist with this — *"You can have your cell phone back once you've studied for an hour!"*

- **_Classes_** Some classes teach you the content of the test; others show you strategies; others do both. Some run two days; others run 14 weeks. Some are outrageously expensive; others are less outrageously expensive. If you go this route, ask for specific data — "You say your average students raise their test scores 400 points. What's the average for students who had PSAT scores like mine?" Also, ask about class scholarships, or discounts, for students from the same high school.

- **_Tutors_** Take your PSAT or PLAN results to an experienced tutor, and in a few sessions, they can work with you on the areas where you most need help. You don't waste time with a class that overviews the whole test, and it can be cheaper than a full-blown class to boot. This works even better if you bring February ACT or SAT results in to prep for the June exams.

- **_Apply to a "No Test" College_** If you think testing doesn't really tell a college anything about you, you're not alone. Over 700 colleges don't use SAT or ACT as part of the admissions process for most of their students. These include some highly selective schools, and the list gets larger every year. If this testing strategy sounds right for you, buzz by *http://www.fairtest.org/optstate.html* to look at the list of schools, then double-check on the Web site of the college you're interested in.

The College Freak Factor is mighty high when it comes to test prep — most students either freak about the tests and do way too much studying, or they freak about having to give up free time and do way too little. You have to do what's comfortable and what you can afford in money and time, but this is the one area where many former students say, "If I had to do anything different, I would have studied more."

Just notice they said study — not obsess.

Chapter 15

SENIOR SCHEDULE AND MORE ON COLLEGE VISITS

By March, you're registered for (or have taken) the ACT and SAT, and you have at least three colleges you'd like to visit. That leaves two things left to do — senior schedule (see *below*), and asking teachers to write you letters of recommendation (see Chapter 18).

Your senior schedule has to do three things:

1. Have all the classes you need to graduate. One key to getting into college is to get out of high school, so double check your transcript; make sure you are literally good to go; and count your gym credits — twice — they're slippery.

2. Keep you challenged all of senior year. Speaking of gym, remember what coach said — play to the whistle. If you take a soft schedule, you'll forget about thinking, studying, writing, and organizing your time. You'll then spend the first semester of college remembering these things, along with learning how to do laundry, getting yourself out of bed, and calling your parents often enough that they'll remember you at Thanksgiving. A bad start in college is like a bad start in 9th grade — it's tough to catch up. You're in shape, so stay in shape — just say no to schedule sludge. If you've run out of tough classes in high school, take some at a local college.

3. Show the colleges you're serious about learning. The trained pigeons schedule hard classes for three years of high school and, maybe, the first half of senior year, but then — out comes six sections of The History of Pizza. The college of your dreams will see this epidemic of senioritis on your final transcript — *yes, you have to send them one* — and if your grades go down a lot (say, A- average to B-), or if your schedule is soft, they'll think you've changed your mind about learning, so they might change their mind about you. Try it if you dare — it happens.

With the goals of junior year behind us, let's revisit visiting colleges. Some students have big dreams about faraway colleges — you wouldn't believe how many juniors ask about University of Hawaii — but they can't get there to visit. In addition, many families can't afford to visit colleges, even if they aren't across the ocean. They can visit the local schools on their list, but the distant ones are a stretch.

Fair enough — it's time for Plans B and C of college visits. Plan B is simple — wait until April of senior year to visit colleges. By then, you'll know which ones you've been admitted to, so the number you'll visit will be smaller. Since this eliminates your ability to see potential colleges as a junior, this plan isn't perfect, but there might be enough local colleges to give you a good taste of the different kinds of colleges that are out there.

Plan C is even simpler — let someone else help pay for it. If one of your pals is heading out for a campus tour by car, offer to pay for gas and go with them. If you're worried their opinion might bias you, talk about that before you go — a true friend will understand, and you'll be able to work something out.

If you're the first in your family to go to college, or a member of an under-represented ethnic group, the college might actually pay for your visit. Fly-in programs are becoming a big deal to even small colleges, and all you have to do is ask and fill out a form. Now that's a bargain.

Chapter 16
MAKING THE LIST

Dudes and dudettes, it's time to chill. Put on your favorite workout shorts; grab a box of cereal; borrow one of your mom's scented candles (no, dude — not the one that plugs into the wall); put on your John Coltrane CD, and crash on the couch.

At this stage of things, you're heading into the home stretch. By studying hard, giving back, thinking about your place in the world and having fun, your high school years have been *da bomb* and *da bedrock* — something to build on, not just for a college application, but for applying yourself once you're in college, and once you're out. Because you built up over time, you're not burned out over college; because your parents and your counselor are in the queue (that's an SAT word!), they're not on your case; because you've visited colleges, you're focused on finding one that's right for you, instead of finding one that's "right."

You'll need to hold on to that last thought really tight from now until next June. Lots of well-meaning folks at the family reunion, the church barbecue or the Custard Cone will ask you where you're going to go and what you're going to major in. If you don't give them the answer they want to hear — that you'll be majoring in business at a name college — they will do things with their face you could have sworn were limited to cartoon characters who eat too many Cocoa Doodles for breakfast. (*Go easy on those, OK?*)

Of course, it's fine to major in business at a name college — if that's what's right for you — but if that's not where you are, then that's not where you should go. Don't get me wrong — the last thing you want to do is head to college without thinking about your plans. But if you've thought about your plans and you don't have a major, then finding a college that will let you look around awhile *is* a plan, even if it's at a college no one's heard of, and even if you change your major a lot once you're there (which most students do — even the business majors).

— 36 —

Keeping your focus amid all of those opinions, mosquitoes and charred burgers might not be easy — so you need to focus on something else. As you start your transition summer, as you continue to visit colleges, remember your goal is to come to the first day of senior year with two things:

1. a killer tan (cool — but use sun screen!);

2. a list of six to eight colleges you'd like to apply to, which includes:
    a. at least one college in your home state;
    b. two colleges with average grades and test scores that are equal to yours, or even a little lower;
    c. a couple of dream schools you can't quite figure out how you'll get into or pay for;
    d. all colleges you'd be happy to go to.

We'll talk more about the list over the next few chapters as I offer you some ideas about college options you probably haven't considered. For now, dream on, be strong in the work you have done so far ...

... And blow out that candle, ace; that pine smell is doing me in!

P.S. *Thirty-one words to go till this chapter hits 600 words. Use the space to write down your current list, and look at it every day this summer.*

Chapter 17
SAFETY SCHOOLS AND TRANSFERRING

Most students don't beef about applying to an in-state school. If you've visited local campuses, you've probably found a college that will work for you if you stay close to home, either to be near family, or because in-state public schools are a bargain. You might have the heart of a Rainbow Warrior (*remember that University of Hawaii thing?*), but hearts are funny things, and by April being a Sooner or a Spartan or a Hustlin' Quaker may be just as wonderful, even though home is just an hour away — or because home is just an hour away.

The real hustle I get (with Quakers or not) is when I tell students to apply to two safety schools — places where, based on test scores and GPA, you're in the middle of the pack, if not a little ahead. Students find nice ways to express their concern about this, but it basically boils down to this:

> "Holmes, why would I want to go to a school where I'm the smartest student?"

I get that. Good students want challenge, and they think the best way to get challenge is from students who are smarter than they are. Other students think a degree from a college nobody's heard of won't help much when it comes to landing jobs or getting into med school.

So why safety schools? First, knowing you've found a college you like and can get into (and a safety school has to be both) gives you confidence — it's the rock you build on while completing applications to more selective colleges. September might tell you it's cool just to apply to tough schools, but February and March seem colder than usual if every application that might be a yes could just as easily (or more likely) be a no. Safety schools school you on how applications work, and give you the "Yes!" factor you need to take on applications with 86 parts.

Second, dough and prestige (*no ma'am, that's one reason, not two — but thanks for asking!*). Lots of competitive colleges offer automatic scholarships to students with high grades or test scores. Right — you get bucks no matter who you are, whether you need them or not. In addition, a student who's stronger than most can find their way into a good college's honors program or advanced scholars courses. This means smaller classes, better profs and fellow students who can rip it up in the classroom. You're looking for someone to set the pace and programs with grad school horsepower? Gentledudes, start your engines!

Finally, there's the two-college strategy. Highly-selective colleges are crazy competitive — the main reason students get rejected is because the college runs out of room. Since very small differences make the difference, some students make a different plan — start at a safety school, and transfer to the dream school.

You have to be careful here — most highly-competitive colleges are even harder to get into as a transfer, and you have to watch the classes you take at School #1, since not all will transfer. This also means you have to go through the application process twice, and deadlines for transfers are different. Still, this is a growing trend — stay local, stoke the GPA, save some dough, and off you go. Also, if you transfer enough college credits, they might not look at your high school grades at all — and sometimes a new start is very cool. Transfer is also an option if your dream school turns out to be a nightmare. Either way, watch your classes, stay organized, get great grades ....

... And, hustle on, Quakers!

Chapter 18

COMMUNITY COLLEGES AND GRADE POINT AVERAGES

Another player in the two-college game is community colleges.

OK, OK. Are you through now?

> *"Junior college? Isn't that where they teach, like, dog grooming and motorcycle safety?"*

First of all, they usually aren't called junior colleges anymore — if you're looking for someone to say that name was a bad idea, my hand is raised. Second, yes, some CCs do teach dog grooming and cake decorating (*hopefully, not in the same classroom at the same time*) …

… And you should be very glad they do. Community colleges were based on this wacky notion that learning shouldn't be over at 22. Time goes by, and people change; the job you loved at 25 is boring at thirty-four, or doesn't pay enough, or is gone. More school.

You thought school was dull, so you got a job after high school and made a ton of money. But now the magic of money has faded (*it does that, youngsters*), and you've found something you really want to do. More school.

You're at a four-year college, but you can't get all of your required classes. Summer vacation is coming up, but you want to get back on track to finish your degree on time. More school.

Lots of people in your community have a need for more school. The needs aren't the same, but the need for a local college *is* the same — that's why everyone voted for special taxes to build a college that's down the street and dirt cheap, with classes that give people new hobbies, new careers, new outlooks on life, and transferable credits to four-year colleges (who often give CC transfer students with good grades great scholarships). From working on your GPA to working to make a dream come true, community colleges can be your best friend for now and for life — and learning for life is what this book is all about.

So no more woofin' about community colleges — dog!

And now, it's time to learn about GPA.

Your high school may have a grading system that requires the average person to use two calculators and a blender to figure out a GPA. As in, Honors classes add .3, Bs in AP® courses add .28, Bs in Honors AP courses add .32, Cs in Accelerated Honors AP courses taught in the Winter semester, lose .46 …

A college wants to compare all students using the same grading system, so they have to take out the different things high schools do to grades and treat them all the same. This is great, except that one college's version of "same" is different from another college's version of "same" — just like high school grading scales are different from one another.

Confused? Join the club.

As they think about senior schedule, students ask if getting Bs in AP classes is better than As in regular classes. If you look at the college options as a group, the answer is, "It depends." If you look at my answer in Chapter 3, the answer is to take the most challenging classes you can. Unless you have one "dream school" that has a special GPA formula, I'd stick with Chapter 3.

Also — if a college says it's looking for a GPA of 3.5, that's based on whatever formula the college uses. This is one reason why students with 3.3s shouldn't hesitate to apply to a 3.5 college — you never know what your recalculated GPA will look like, unless you understand the way all of your colleges will treat your grades.

(*Of course, if you do know, skip college and go work for NASA — you're rocket scientist material!*)

Chapter 19
APPLICATION DEADLINES

In addition to thinking about instate schools, safety schools, transfer schools and GPAs, you might want to think about applying to a college based on when you'll hear back from them. This menu has five different entrees:

- **_First Come, First Served (Rolling Admissions)_** The sooner your application is complete at a rolling admissions college, the sooner they will read it and make a decision. If you'd like some security in your senior year, you might want to consider applying to a safety school that's rolling — in some cases, you can hear by October if you apply in September.

- **_First Come, First Served, Sort of (Early Action or EA)_** EA gives you an early date — usually November 1st — to turn in a completed application. All applications received by that date are read together, and decisions go out before Christmas. With EA, you hear earlier, but you still have until May 1st to decide if you want to go there.

- **_First Committed, First Served (Early Decision or ED)_** ED is like EA, but with a REALLY important addition. Like EA, you apply early, and you hear early. However, if you apply ED and are accepted, you MUST ATTEND THAT COLLEGE. Once an ED school says yes, you withdraw your applications to all other colleges. The only exception (and this is only sometimes) is if the college can't meet all of your financial need. If they can, you've found your new home.

- **_First Come And First Committed, First Served (Early Action Single Choice)_** EA Single Choice is just like EA, except a college that offers EA Single Choice limits the number of EA applications you can make to one — just them. If the college takes you, you still have until May 1st to decide to go there — but you are limiting your EA choices by applying to that school.

- **_Y'all Come, Y'all Served (Regular Admissions)_** These programs establish a common deadline (usually January 1st), and all applications are read at the same time. Decisions usually come out around April 1st.

Since some colleges have both an early program and a regular program, you might have to figure out which way to apply. Early programs give you the advantage of showing a college you're really interested in them, especially an ED application — but of course, if ED takes you, you have to go, and that commitment might be too big for you. In addition, many colleges take a large number of students from early programs, where the number of applications is small — so applying early may be to your advantage. In addition, some early applicants may be deferred, where the college decides to review you with the later applicants. You may get in later, but you may not.

If you get the impression that figuring out the math of early programs is as complicated as the math of recalculating GPAs, you're on the right track. Advice on applying early varies greatly from college to college, but the general rule of thumb is you should apply early if a school is a top choice for you — in the case of an ED application, _THE choice_. Since many colleges with early programs are dropping them, this may be less of a big deal soon; either way, I'd find at least one safety school that does rolling admission, get that admission letter in my back pocket, and then take on the math of early versus regular.

No matter the program, remember that deadlines are **stone-cold real**. An application that's due January 1st won't get read if it's postmarked January 2nd — so plan ahead.

Chapter 20
COLLEGE COSTS

Now that you're working on your final list, you (or your parents) are probably thinking about paying for college. This is bad, bad, good and bad …

It's bad if you decide not to scope out a school or apply just because you think it costs too much. You visit colleges to find out as much about you and what you like as you do to find out about the college. A trip to Megabucks College could lead to the discovery that you love archaeology, and that can lead you to dig up (*get it — archaeology? dig up?*) other great archaeology schools that cost less. If you don't make the trip, you don't discover a part of yourself — talk about a high price!

It's also bad to pass on the high end, because the high end might be cheaper. A parent called me to scold me for encouraging her senior to apply to a college they couldn't afford and urged me to "encourage" their daughter to go to a local public college instead. The pricey school was perfect for the student, and she applied, hoping to get one of the college's full scholarships. There were only 10 available, but that didn't matter, because she only needed the one she got — and suddenly, school was free.

At the same time, it's good to build your list of colleges with money in mind. The student did indeed apply to that affordable public college and would have been happy there — a perfect safety school. A few big-cost colleges on your list is fine; all big-cost colleges means you might be looking more at name and prestige than the things that really matter, like major, fit and reality. Dream? You bet — but a dream is just one kind of vision, and putting together a good list requires insights of many kinds.

Finally, it's bad if now is the first time your parents are considering how to pay for college. Like most big expenses, planning ahead is good, even though doing that is often more jarring than putting it off and hoping things will work out — because sometimes, they don't. If your parents have a financial planner — no, that wouldn't be Al the lottery ticket guy at Speedy Mart — it's long past time for a visit. They should set up a meeting, without you, right away; in fact, that's a good idea for parents who have planned ahead, too. Mention it at your next weekly meeting …

… And take along *www.finaid.org* with you. There's a lot to know — that you have to file with the Federal Government to get anything from just about anyone, that you can't file with the Feds until after January 1st of senior year, that your college has other forms to fill out, that too much loan is bad. *Finaid.org* will get you through it all, in simple language, along with the biggest scholarship database in the history of the planet. You fill out a survey, give them your e-mail and *voila!* — you get a list of (usually) 200 scholarships you can apply for. When new scholarships come in, or scholarship deadlines are coming up, they e-mail you to let you know. They also have some great articles about scholarships scams, and why you should never have to pay to be eligible for a scholarship or to find out about them.

It's true that money is a tool with power — but so is a chain saw, and that isn't getting in your way of finding a great school. Like all power tools, treat it with respect, and you'll be fine.

Chapter 21
LETTERS OF RECOMMENDATION — THE BIG PICTURE

Now that your list is complete, it's time to get busy. Not every college requires letters of recommendation — in fact, there are more that don't want letters than those that do. At the same time, having at least one letter of recommendation (I recommend two) is a good idea.

- It may help you get admitted. Colleges that don't ask for letters usually don't mind if you send one. If you're applying to a college where your grades and test scores make you a "maybe," extra words of support from a teacher who knows you well are right there for the admissions committee to consider — and those can push you over the top.

- You may change your mind soon. Suppose you stop by a college on your way home from Aunt Marge's over Thanksgiving weekend, and you love the place — but it requires letters of recommendation and has a December 1st deadline. If you plan ahead for the possible, your letters are waiting for you, and your dream stays alive.

- You may change your mind later on. If you transfer colleges or put college off for a while, your college may still want recommendations from high school. If you ask the teachers to write those letters now, they'll write about you based on fresh memories, not based on how they remember you two years from now — and for as much as they like you, time can make a difference.

- You may need it for money. Once you're through applying for colleges, you'll probably be filling out scholarship applications. Many scholarship applications require letters of recommendation, and having one that's ready to go can make all the difference in finding cash for college.

Some students freak about asking for letters — it's easy. In the spring of junior year, you've asked your teachers privately if they would write you a good letter of recommendation. The word "good" is important — any teacher can write you a letter, but if it's just going to be a list of your accomplishments and grades, that won't help. You want a letter from someone who knows you as a person and as a student — that makes a good letter. If the teacher honestly feels they can't write you a good letter, they'll tell you that in a gentle way. Don't be crushed — they're really helping you, since weak letters of recommendation are usually worse than no letters at all …

… And this goes back to looking at the big picture. Just like applying to college isn't just about college, asking teachers for letters of recommendation isn't just about filling out forms. If you've really been making the most of high school, if you've been living and learning instead of only getting good grades, you're sure to have at least two or three teachers who didn't simply grade your papers and check your attendance. You'll also have learned about life from mentors, the teachers you formed relationships with, the ones who kept an eye out for you, who taught you right from wrong, or something else about the way the world worked.

You won't feel close to all of your teachers (and vice versa), but if spring of junior year comes around, and you have no teachers who know at least a little bit about your soul, that's bad, not because it looks bad to the colleges, but because you'll have missed a chance to grab onto life, give of yourself, and learn from the masters — and that kind of wisdom is simply too good to miss.

Chapter 22

LETTERS — THE NUTS AND BOLTS

As you think about the teachers who know you best, you also need to see if your colleges require letters from specific teachers. Most colleges will let you decide which teachers to choose, but some will ask for a letter from an English teacher, or a teacher you had in a class related to your major. (Engineering schools often ask for a letter from a math teacher, and art schools from an art teacher.) It's good to have one letter from someone who can talk about your writing ability — that's often an English teacher, but it doesn't have to be (unless the college requires it).

If the college asks for two letters, sending three is OK, as long as you're pretty sure the third letter won't repeat what's in the other two. Students often send a third letter from a coach or a rabbi or a boss (or even a third teacher) that shows another side of the student, and that's great — as long as the ideas are fresh. But don't stretch it — it's pretty hard to justify sending four letters when two are asked for, and six are out of the question.

Once your letter writers give you the OK, thank them and let them know when you'll need the letter. In some cases, you might have a September deadline, and a good letter takes about three weeks to prepare. By giving your writers plenty of time to prepare, you are giving them the respect they are due, and you are helping them to help you — that's why you ask in spring of the junior year.

If the colleges have recommendation forms your writers must complete, fill out the top part of the forms with your name, etc. You'll want to give these forms to your letter writers in the fall of your senior year — it's OK for them to submit the same letter to different colleges, but the forms are different and need to be filled out individually. If your high school wants the letter writers to mail their letters directly to the college, give your writers envelopes addressed to the college with **two** stamps on them. This way, each writer completes the form, encloses a copy of the letter, and drops it in the mail …

… Because you aren't supposed to see the letters. In asking for a letter of recommendation, you are asking a teacher to write a letter about you, not to write a letter to you. If this is a shock to you, get used to it; you'll soon fill out job applications where employers will want to talk to friends and former bosses without your knowing what they'll say. Some colleges will ask if you want to see the letters after you're admitted; the choice is up to you, but experience tells me teachers generally write stronger letters if they know the student will never see it (*don't ask me why*).

Be sure to send a thank you note to your writers right after the application deadline has passed. In addition, be sure to follow up with your letter writers after you hear back from your colleges (whether you get admitted or not); you asked them to write a letter for you because they care about you, so they'll be curious to know how things worked out. Telling them or e-mailing them is OK, but teachers still prefer hand-written notes from their students — that's part of the relationship that goes beyond filling out a few forms, so of course, that's the best way to go.

Chapter 23
LINING UP AN INTERVIEW

While many colleges require letters of recommendation, far fewer require interviews. Most students breath a sigh of relief when they hear this, and I don't know why — after all, why wouldn't you want someone at the college of your dreams to hear about your dreams? More about that later — for now ...

If a college requires an interview, you can fulfill this requirement one of two ways, and either way has its advantages. You can conduct an interview on campus — this is nice, because it means you'll have a chance to see campus as well, which is really a must before you attend a college. If you get an on-campus interview, it will most likely be with the person who will be reading your application, which is always a bonus.

The other way you fulfill this requirement is through an interview with a graduate of the school, known hereafter as alumni. These interviews are usually local, so they can be built around your schedule. The alumni who conduct these interviews are trained by the college, so they know how to conduct an interview and often offer some good insights into life at the college as a student, which is great to know.

If you want to interview on campus, you have to call the college — and most interview times fill up quickly (*like, by fall*), so call in July. If the college requires an interview, and you can't make it to campus, the local alumni will call you to set up the meeting. If you come home and find a request for an interview on your voice mail, **return the call within 24 hours**. Work out a time and date that works for both of you. In addition, if this is an alumni interview, you need to arrange a place to meet, which should be a public place that offers relative privacy (like a coffee shop).

The day before the interview, make sure you confirm the date, time and place — this way, everyone knows when the interview will take place. You confirm the meeting by calling either the college or the alumni; if you get voice mail, simply leave your name, the date, time and place where the meeting will occur, and a phone number where someone can call you if they have questions. This shows both courtesy and organization on your part — in general, colleges like both.

OK — now the big question — what to wear. Because this is an interview, and not a fashion show, you don't have to spend hours thinking about this —just look nice, and you'll be fine. For guys, this means a collared shirt and dark or khaki slacks and something other than sandals or sneakers; a few years ago, even liberal thinkers were telling guys not to wear earrings to interviews, but now there are reports of male interviewers wearing them — so, there's some room to negotiate here, but I'd leave them at home, and put on a tie. For girls, this means a dressier, non-revealing top, slacks or a skirt (true confession here — I really think a skirt of knee length or longer leaves a better impression) and shoes that complement the outfit. Having said all of this, I know many students who had great interviews in T-shirts and jeans — while I'm not recommending that, I point it out just to say this isn't the part of the interview to lose sleep over …

… And speaking of sleep, get lots the night before. *Risky Business* aside, interviews don't occur at parties, and good ones don't occur after parties.

Chapter 24
SHOWTIME

OK — so you've confirmed the appointment, and you aren't dressed like a refugee. Good.

You want to arrive for interview early — at least five minutes early. This gives you a chance to catch your breath, get comfortable with where you'll interview and a minute for the rest room, if you need it. If you get lost on the way, CALL if you can. Being lost is not grounds for being denied admission; being gracious about getting lost is the thoughtful thing to do and demonstrates your humanity to the interviewer. If the interviewer arrives after you do, stand up, say hello, smile and offer your hand.

The key to all of this is to just be yourself — really. The interviewer will probably ask you open-ended questions — questions where you will have to supply more than a "yes" or "no" answer. Typical questions are, "Why are you interested in our college?;" "What's the most interesting thing you've done?;" or the famous, "Tell us about yourself." Your answers should be complete and of a good length — about a minute or so. Keep the rules of a good college essay in mind — answer the question, show warmth, humor, intellect and grace in your answers (easy on the humor — don't force a funny moment), and show the personal side of yourself without getting too personal. If you want to relate a story you told as part of your essay, that's fine, but don't make it the entire answer to a question — this is a chance to **add** to your application, **not duplicate** it.

If you're having an interview that isn't required, you've asked for the meeting — so now is the time to get down to business. If you want to talk about the unusual circumstances you've faced as a student (illness, family issues, boredom with school) and how you've overcome them, tell your story; if you've taken the tour and have additional questions (that you've written down in advance), fire away; if you're meeting to show interest in the college, talk about what makes you unique, where you think you want to go in life, and what you have to give to the college. The idea is to take charge while being gracious, to give the meeting substance without being lengthy and to show the interviewer why the college can't exist without you. Keep those three things in mind, and you'll do well.

In a required interview, you'll be asked if you have any questions. It's good to think about one or two in advance — like, the day before the interview. If you happen to think of one on the spot, that's great too — the advanced questions are just in case. These questions should require answers that aren't in the college catalog or brochure — remember, the quality of the question can show the thought and interest you've put in to investigating the college. You can also ask your alumni interviewer about their perceptions of the college; while the answer you get is just their perspective, it's still good information to have as you consider the best place to be.

When the interview is over, stand up, thank the interviewer, shake hands, and off you go. It is exceptionally good form to call or e-mail the interviewer the next day to thank them for the interview and invite them to please contact you if they have any other questions. I think it's a better idea to hand write a note, but the phone call or e-mail is my concession to modernity, and it still conveys a sense of gratitude most students don't extend.

Chapter 25
ESSAYS

I don't know why students freak about essays. Colleges give you a couple of months to write them; you can get a little help with them if you want — and they're all about YOU. Yes, this is the part where the show is all yours, where it's focused on Numero Uno, the Big Enchilada, the person you like so much, you put their reflection in the mirror every time you look into one.

That last one made ya think, didn't it?

That may sound selfish, but it's actually the key to writing an effective essay — be you. Most colleges give you a very general topic to write on, where you get to steer the ship. If the questions are specific, you answer them in a way that shows them who you are. Some ground rules:

- Answer the question. It's great to write a broad answer that serves as a window into your life, but if they want to know a person who inspired you, tell them. If you read your answer, and it's not clear to you who inspired you, the college will have no clue either — time to start over.

- Answer the question honestly. Don't say your father because you think it will move them, and don't say Barnacle Bob just to be cute. The essay is a guided tour of your mind, life, vision and soul — what you are, not what you think you're supposed to be. Show them the real deal.

- Watch the humor. An Ivy League rep once said if you could get him to laugh out loud while reading your application, you were in. Trouble is, lots of students try — and fail. What's funny to you may be dull, trite, pathetic or strange to the committee. As a rule, try for warm and spirited — let Chris Rock do shtick.

- Watch the content. Trite (an essay on deciding what the essay should be about), pathetic ("I'm not worthy — but take me anyway") or strange ("I'm really a vampire") are generally out. What you have to say should be an honest look at you, but this is an introduction, not the tenth week of therapy. Be focused and balanced, and you'll do fine.

- Show it to an English teacher. You know at least one English teacher who loves to slash essays with red pen — grammar, spelling, the whole tour. This is your new best friend; bring them your rough draft and chocolate, and let the games begin.

- Write the essay yourself. The essay is indeed a guided tour of your life — as written by you. Having someone else do "significant editing" is your first act of college-level plagiarism, and it may be your last. Don't.

- Repeat yourself. You can use the same essay for different colleges, as long as the essay answers the question and shows something about you. You'll need to take the names of other colleges out (Don't tell Brown, "I've always wanted to go to Dartmouth"), and you want to put specifics in about the new college ("It's great that Chicago requires its students to swim. When I was six …"), but other than that, cut and copy away.

Colleges would love to put you up for two weeks to really get to know you — but if they did that for everyone, you'd be 45 before they admitted you. The essay takes the place of that two weeks — write it so that when they read it, they feel like you just left the room, and your chair is still warm.

Chapter 26
THE FINAL CHECK

With the essays written, you're in the home stretch. A few final touches:

- Almost every college has a secondary school report form, asking for an official transcript and/or counselor comments. These forms go to your counselor AT LEAST a month before they are due. Check to see what your school's policy is, then fill out the top and hand them in. If the college wants your grades from the first half of senior year, turn that form in as well.

- I'm hoping you checked your transcript for incorrect or missing grades when you met with your counselor in February. If not, check now — nothing ruins an application like a D in Calculus you never got.

- Use your resources wisely. It's good news if an app's due January 1st, (you can work on it over break), but your counselor won't be in the office December 28th, so make sure you have all the info you need from school on the last day of school. **ATTENTION ALL STUDENTS**: Even if you have access to your counselor's home number, don't call them. They love you, but the absence of your planning isn't their emergency. Unless they tell you otherwise, make your best guess, send it in, then see if your counselor needs to help you fix it the first day back.

- Have someone look over your application to make sure it's complete. You can earn big "sweetie" points if you let your parents do this during your weekly meeting — but they are checking the form *you* completed, not filling it out for you.

- Finally, if the college requires official test scores and you haven't sent them, go to *www.collegeboard.com* (SATs) or *www.act.org* (ACT), and order them *now*.

If you're mailing out apps two days or less from the deadline (online apps are better), go to the post office and watch them get postmarked (bring the MP3 player along — the line is serpentine in December).

After a day (or five) of resting from application frenzy, it's time to re-join the living. Waiting to hear from a college is like waiting to be asked out on a date — the more you stay home, the longer until the phone rings. It's the last six months of senior year, so there has to be something on the "to do" list you're dying to get to — get busy.

In addition, don't look back. As a 9th grader, you wanted perfect grades, smoked SATs, universal acclaim as The Ruler of Community Service, and an admissions letter from Harvard engraved in gold. Maybe you got those things, maybe you didn't; either way, if the last app goes in the mail and you've done everything you could to make it all work, there's nothing else that can be added — except keep living a rich, full life.

You can't tell what decisions the mail will bring from colleges — yes, no, maybe — but it won't bring a decision about you as a person; life is what you make it, not what college you go to. My dad told me there are two ways to make your life shorter: Try and make all the green lights, and think about what you should have done. We're here for long life, so don't do either — be grateful for the chances you've had; know you've built a great life for yourself; and look ahead.

P.S. *If a college says they're missing something, don't freak — contact the right person (teacher, counselor, yourself) and send it in immediately. Mail gets lost, but it's OK; you're getting a do-over. Send it in, and move on.*

Chapter 27
THREE KINDS OF DECISIONS

When you hear from a college, you'll get one of *four* decisions:

- **Admission** Also known as the "thick" envelope, the offer of admissions includes information on housing, orientation and financial aid. Be sure to read all of it; this information will be of great value to you if you need to decide among several offers of admission.

- **Conditional Admission** Colleges offer you a seat in the freshman class with a requirement — generally, that you participate in a tutoring or student support program, that your first semester grades are at a certain level, or that you come to campus over the summer to participate in a college readiness program. These offers of admission are not an "either/or" proposition — if you want to go to that college, you must satisfy the requirements outlined in the offer of admission.

- **Not Offered Admission** News that a college cannot offer you admission usually comes in a thin envelope. As I said before, colleges mean it when they say they wish they could offer you admission, and they value your work as a student; it's just that colleges simply run out of room. As I also said before, admissions decisions aren't a judgment on your life — they just can't take everyone.

I'm sometimes asked if an admissions decision can be appealed. Just like every college handles admissions decisions differently, every college handles appeals differently — and remember, colleges do not have to offer any kind of appeal at all. In general, follow these guidelines:

Read your letter closely. These letters often explain both the procedures you need to follow to file an appeal and the things colleges look for in reviewing an appeal. If your letter gives you no indication, call the office of admission and ask what their appeal policy is — and remember that some colleges will not take appeals except (or even) in very rare circumstances.

See if you can find out why you were denied admission in the first place. A conversation with an admissions officer may give the college enough additional information about you to form the basis of an appeal. If the college needs more information, you can ask for details on what the college would like to see — or, in some cases, you can find out if an appeal would not be the best use of your time.

Generally speaking, colleges will look at an appeal closely if you can provide additional information above and beyond what you included in your original application that shows you are a strong and/or unique student. Seventh semester grades, progress reports from your current classes, additional letters of recommendation, a supporting paragraph or two from your counselor, previously unexplained circumstances — these kinds of things can make a difference.

Remember that a successful appeal depends on a variety of factors — your strength as a student, what you've been doing with your life since you applied (see?), your continued interest in the college, the number of spaces the college has available, etc. In some cases, continued interest and strong grades may be enough to get you in on appeal — but in some cases, it won't.

An appeal isn't a sure thing, and the extra energy it requires to put an appeal together — not just yours, but the energy of your counselor, your teachers, and the college — can be high at this busy time of year. Before you start an appeal, be sure to think about your chances of success and your real interest in the college, and let your answers guide you accordingly.

Those are the three simple possibilities. *The toughie comes next.*

Chapter 28
WAITLISTS

A letter indicating you've been waitlisted usually comes all by itself. The letter indicates that the college is still considering your application, but must hear from the admitted students first before they may — again, that's may — offer you admission.

This is tricky for two reasons. First, it's tough to wait longer; you were ready to hear yes or no, and you got "give us a little longer." Many students just can't live with the uncertainty anymore; if that's you, thank the college, say you're not interested, and move on.

Second, waitlist rules vary greatly by college — so ...

- Re-read the letter from the college to see if it gives you any information about the wait-list — how the order is determined, when it is determined, and what you need to do to stay on it. If all of the admitted soccer players turn down College X and College Y, College X may go to the waitlist only for soccer players, whereas College Y may simply start offering admission to the students at the top of the list, whether they play soccer or not (and risk a lousy season). Find out if you're dealing with an X or Y.

- If this information isn't in the letter, call the college and ask. They may give you some suggestions; if they do, write them down, since they are basically telling you how to improve your chances of moving up on the list.

Next, it's decision time. Given the college options you have, do you still feel it's worth pursuing this college as a possible option? As you think about this, it's **very** important to ask two questions ...

1. If a slot doesn't open up at this college, what college will I select?

2. If a slot does open up at this college, what college will I select?

If the answer to these questions is the same, you're done here — move on. If your decision depends in part on financial aid, remember that the amount of aid available to students who come off the waitlist is usually limited. Colleges offer all of their aid to admitted students first; as a result, the aid available to waitlisted students is limited to the amount of aid turned down by admitted students. That's no reason to pack it in — it's just something to consider, or ask about.

If you decide to go for it, don't be shy. "I want you to know I am still very interested in attending College X this fall" sends a clear statement of where you stand; if College X is your first choice, you can say that, too (but remember, only one first choice). Grades in current classes, additional awards and activities, maybe another letter — all of that may help, but don't drive them crazy, and tell the truth. Send in one complete packet of new material as soon as it's ready, then call or e-mail about two weeks after that.

Most colleges won't review their waitlist until after May 1st, which is when students are expected to notify one — and only one — college they'll be going there in the fall. If you're still waiting to hear from a waitlisted college on April 30th, put in the required May 1st deposit at another school. If the college of your dreams pulls you off the waitlist later, cancel your admission at the other college in writing — and know you probably won't get your deposit back.

If you want to go for it, give it your all — but remember, you have a life; what you're looking for is a college.

Chapter 29
GENESIS

Tell me the truth — when I told you to apply to six to 10 colleges, you thought I was out. Now it's late April of your senior year, and Chapter 16 has set in — you're not sure what to do.

There are some great ways around this. If you've held off visiting campuses, now is the time. You only have until May 1st, so do what you can with Spring Break and the travel plans of your fellow freshmen seekers. Write a new list of questions, re-visit campuses you've been to, and remember dreams change in six months —and that's OK.

As you do this, don't get caught up in the glow of getting in. Colleges who say yes will call you day and night, some to be helpful, some trying to persuade you. Same deal with financial aid packages; one client picked a school based on a $600 grant they'd given him, just because they called it an honors scholarship. That makes the school cheaper — but does it make it for you? Figure out a way to keep your head clear — run two miles, up the number of parent meetings to one a day, play George Clinton records backwards — and maintain focus …

… Because your focus might see something new. Right about now, some students think about putting college on hold. This is pretty common, and choosing to defer — right, the same word used when colleges ask for more time — has its advantages. Students who defer get the chance to do something they've always wanted to do — see the world, work with the poor, study a language, earn more scratch for college, or maybe just chill. Parents often freak about this choice; they're convinced that once you're out, you won't come back. Colleges don't feel that way — in fact, most colleges let you take a year off and automatically hold a spot for you for the following fall, so long as you ask for a deferral before May 1st of your senior year and promise not to take classes somewhere else.

If you think deferral might be for you, apply to colleges as if you weren't going to defer — the logistics of applying to college are **huge** once you're out of high school — then read *Taking Time Off* by Colin Hall and Ron Lieber. It's better to make a plan for next year while you're still in high school, whether it includes college or not — and no college is a good choice, if it's for the right reason. Making a plan up as you go along spells disaster, so if you're simply avoiding commitment, deferral probably isn't for you.

Once you've seen the schools, focused on what matters, and balanced the greatness of one school with the affordability of another, it's time to put those jammies back on, grab one last handful of Cocoa Doodles, and decide. May 1st is the day you tell one college yes, and thank the others — but it's really only one, and it's really May 1st.

Telling lots of schools yes on May 1st is like saying yes to 10 prom dates — you get more time to choose, but it hurts everyone else. Students stay on waitlists for no reason; colleges schedule classes that won't have enough students; and parents lose deposits that could go for textbooks — or retirement. It's great to have options, but the band is playing, and it's time to dance. Size up your partners, pick the one that will get you across the dance floor with the right balance of support and excitement, and move to the music of the future — your future.

Chapter 30

FOR SOMEDAY (I HOPE NOT)

Sometimes the life you build turns out to be the life you don't want to live after all. If that's where you are someday, I offer this story for you for safekeeping. I hope this lad's adventures do not await you — but in the event a day comes that leaves you wondering about your own capabilities, remember this.

My first client was a wreck. A bright enough boy, with good grades and test scores to boot — but no self-esteem. None. He clung to the sides of the hallway between classes, didn't ask many questions about college, and ended up in the honors college of a public university he had no business going to — for as nice a college as it was for some, he had other things to do, but he didn't know it.

Fall of the freshmen year came, and disaster was right at his heels. Between the blasting stereos and the late night screaming — and this was in the honors dorm — he finally figured out this wasn't the place for him. After two weeks, he packed his bags and headed for home. He managed to get into the fall semester of a nearby commuter college that started late, but he really longed for something different. He re-applied to another residential college, where he figured things might be better; he knew some students who went there, the campus was pretty, and it was big enough for him to be anonymous, just like always.

He headed out for his third college on New Year's Day, less than six months after he'd graduated from high school. After about three weeks, it was pretty clear this place wasn't heaven either, and yet something was different. The stereos weren't as loud — it was winter, after all — and a couple of the teachers talked to him like he was a human being, so he decided this was the place to make his stand. For once, he was going to steer his destiny, and not the other way around.

With that change in attitude, things worked out pretty well. He met up with some high school friends, who invited him to join their intramural basketball and softball teams. (He was awful, but it didn't matter all that much — so were they.) His understanding of classical music impressed a couple of girls enough to get past his low self-esteem and go out on a couple of dates — nothing intense, but certainly reassuring. His academic interests led him to work as an assistant on a research project studying language development among American children — groundbreaking stuff at the time — and he gained the respect of many of his instructors, especially the writing profs, who told him he really had something, if he wanted to work at it.

Twenty-four months after he started at his third college — two and a half years after graduating from high school — he signed his first employment contract. Two days after that, he walked across the commencement stage, not once, but twice, having earned enough credits for two separate degrees, making him the first member of his family to graduate from college, and a working stiff to boot.

Three months after that, he turned 20.

I know you have worked very hard to build the very best future you possibly can. In the event your current plan should go awry, there will be another plan for another day — listen closely; always be receptive to the possible; and know that the choice to succeed is ultimately yours, and yours alone ... but you will never be alone.

Chapter 31
WHAT'S NEXT

I said this book wouldn't be perfect, and I'm sorry to say I was right. We didn't get to a lot of things — athletics, artists, military academies, colleges overseas — but I think we covered enough of the ground rules to give you the big picture. Most people think getting into a good college is about rocket science or tea leaves, when it's really about hard work, focus, curiosity and knowing what it means to take a deep, full breath. Colleges want to know what you've done in the world so far, and what you think your role in the world of tomorrow might be. If you can get that into an application, you'll get into any college that's great for you, and you'll have everything you need to live (*one more time!*) a rich, full life.

As promised, I won't leave you hanging in the wind, unless that's where you choose to be. If you have questions about college, or comments about the book, e-mail them to *collegeisyours@comcast.net*. I'm one of the team of counselors who answers these questions, and we'll do what we can to help you on your way. If you'd like to do your school a favor, tell your counselor MyFootpath makes a great tool to help your whole school make better decisions about college. PrepHQ keeps track of what students applied where and whether they got admitted; it also has a great way of keeping track of scholarships and a communication tool your counselor can use to talk to all 500 of their counselees at once. PrepHQ is great, and best of all, your school can most likely get it for free. If you want to do some real community service, pass *www.myfootpath.com* along to your counselor.

Two more things before class is dismissed. First, you have a pretty good clue about how to choose a college; now, you have to put it in practice. It doesn't matter where you go, when you go, how many you go to, or if you don't go at all — you've got enough here to build a future on something other than hope, what your squeeze is doing about life, or "beats me." Run if you want to — you read the book, and it's too late to pretend you're stupid. Take a breath, catch a dream, and ride it wherever it will take you; you have the skills to hang on, hang in, and hold your head high, because knowledge is freedom ... and in the words of the founders of Roeper School, "with that freedom comes responsibility." As you celebrate senior year, getting into college and graduation, there's a good chance you'll be hanging out at parties and celebrations that are pretty wide open. This is especially true at college, where there will be no bells to remind you about what to do or when to do it, which means the choices are pretty much up to you.

I don't want this to turn into a health class lecture, or (even worse) a political science lecture about the necessity of law; instead, let me remind you of some ideas you probably already know:

- Developmentally, you aren't through growing yet, and the fine tuning your body is doing now requires as few pollutants as possible. In addition, many of you may still be in a developmental phase where the use of drugs and alcohol now could create a dependency that will be difficult to shake, not just now, but ever — so yes, 20 is different from 21.

- The later it gets, the better the chance the guy driving next to you is drunk. It's an old statistic, but I once read that one out of every three cars on the road after 11pm on the weekend — one out of every three — is being driven by a legally-drunk driver.

- Legally, drunk driving, possession of alcohol by a minor, furnishing alcohol to a minor, and possession and sale of illegal drugs to anyone are crimes. If convicted, this information can be devastating to a college application as well as applications for loans, employment, military service — and lives beyond just yours.

As a counselor, part of my job is to help you create the best future you can possibly have; to that end, from now until forever, do the following:

- Do not, under any circumstance, get in a car driven by a drunk driver (any drunk driver), or in a car where alcohol or drugs are being used. Both are unsafe; with the latter, you'll go to jail, and with the former, you could end up hurt, or worse.

- If you're driving after 11pm, plan a route home that gets you past the fewest number of bars and restaurants as possible.

- If offered a substance that is unsafe, unwise, or illegal for you to use, graciously say no. If being gracious is impossible, you have some place better to be, and truer friends to be with — pull out your car keys, or make that call, and move on.

Blind obedience to stupid laws is questionable — I think life teaches us all that. However, obedience to a law you may not fully understand is a different thing. You've worked hard to build a bright future — do yourself and the world a favor, stick around to live it out, and I promise you that one day the law you might not fully understand will make stone-cold sober perfect sense …

… And if you think I'm saying that just because it's my job, let me point out this is the only chapter that's over 600 words. Way over.

I guess I'm busted.

Don't you be.

Chapter 32
600 WORDS FOR PARENTS

Dudes and dudettes, this bit is just for the folks.

Really.

So go already!

Thank you for the interest you're taking in your child's life — and in their college choice. I'd like to think I know the college selection process well, but you're a clear expert about your child (hopefully, second only to them). With the right balance of ideas and participation from you and me, your son or daughter will have the best possible foundation to build a great college choice on.

I have a couple of suggestions to make this process work well for you. First, you really do need to see yourself as an expert. You might not know everything about your child, but your willingness to use what you know and let them teach you more will make a huge difference — before, during and after college.

Second, you need to see this process in a way that makes sense to you. If you've never had a child choose a college, or if it's been a while, you'll see it's very different from when you chose a college — there's more information, more preparation and more choice. It's like the difference between buying a house in a buyer's market or a seller's market — the product is the same, but the rules are very different.

As you read this book and work with your child, I hope you'll use your house/apartment hunting experience as a model. Like house hunting, it's great to see pictures, do Internet research, and run spreadsheets on colleges — but the way you know a house will really work is to see it, feel it, and take it in. You don't always (or ever) find the perfect house, but you start with a list of what it has to have, go out looking, maybe change the list a little, find a few that will work — and a first choice emerges. After doing more research, running a cost analysis, lining up financing and just letting things sink in, you put in an offer and see how it lines up with that of other bidders. If it all works out, you're in; if not, you've got another house that will be just as nice, only in a different way.

In a nutshell, that's the college selection process — just don't try to explain it that way to teenagers, since their experience in house buying is a little slim.

Third, do everything you can to let your child own this experience. Your athletic daughter didn't make the select travel team by letting you try out, and your son the all-state oboe player didn't make the audition by having you practice for him. As with all things, your emotional and logistical support is vital to this process — but be careful to let them lead. Chapter 9 talks about *the* tried and true way to maintain a good balance of your interest and their independence. Start at the beginning of the book, then enjoy that chapter when it comes up — unless you're already planning to fill out the college applications for your child, in which case you should read that chapter now, and develop Plan B for the applications.

Parents of college-bound students often say fear, a lack of knowledge, or love for their child is what motivates them in helping their children find a college. In 22 years of doing this, I can tell you the only successful, supportive relationships in the college selection process are the ones built on love. Let that be the one and only motive behind all you do, and all will go well.

About The Roeper School

George and Annemarie Roeper came to the United States shortly before World War II to escape the horrors of Nazi Germany. In 1941 they opened a school in Detroit designed to create an atmosphere of mutual trust and respect between teachers and students. The Roepers believed a school based on those principles would teach children to embrace all of their relationships — with their families, their peers and the world — with the same blend of humanity and equality. The school became a school for gifted children in 1956, when George and Annemarie determined gifted children were most receptive to this message of support and acceptance of different talents and interests.

With two campuses located in suburban Detroit, The Roeper School is recognized as a worldwide leader in gifted education in a climate rich with social responsibility. Over 600 children attend the school in grades nursery through 12 representing one of the most diverse student populations in Michigan. Since its first high school graduating class in 1969, Roeper alumni have gone on to serve their communities and the world in a variety of ways. Alumni include an Oscar® winner, the holder of patents for the Microsoft Windows® operating system, and two Jeopardy!® champions, along with dozens of alumni who have quietly worked as doctors, lawyers, publishers, artists, teachers, business professionals and parents to instill the same balance of cooperation, freedom and responsibility in the world that is the hallmark of a Roeper education.

The content of this handbook is almost identical to the information provided as part of the college counseling curriculum at Roeper. Where changes were required to make the ideas useful to a broader audience, every effort was made to maintain the same tone of inquiry and support that is Roeper.

You can find out more about The Roeper School, including information on summer programs available for all students and *The Roeper Review*, a journal on gifted education, at *www.roeper.org*.

About NACAC

The National Association for College Admission Counseling (NACAC) is a nonprofit organization dedicated to helping colleges, high schools, parents and students work together to make the best college decisions for students. Founded in 1937, NACAC provides a wide variety of workshops, conferences, publications and leadership experiences for high school counselors and college admission professionals. NACAC also hosts dozens of national college fairs and offers a wide number of publications to help parents and students better understand college options and financial aid.

NACAC's *Statement of Principles of Good Practice* (SPGP) is widely viewed as the authoritative guide for the fair, professional and ethical conduct of the college selection process. A companion piece, the *Statement of Students' Rights and Responsibilities in the College Admission Process*, gives students and families a clear guide to follow as they apply to colleges and decide which college to attend. There are many other publications, workshops and efforts NACAC creates and supports to help make sure that all students who want to go to college can go to college.

With 9,000 members working in the college admissions field throughout the world, NACAC has something to offer anyone interested in learning more about college opportunities. For more information on NACAC's services, including a schedule of NACAC's national college fairs, visit *http://www.nacacnet.org*.

About the Author

Patrick O'Connor is on the Political Science Faculty of Oakland Community College and is Director of College Counseling at The Roeper School, both in Metropolitan Detroit. Born and raised in Detroit, he has been a college counselor since 1984, serving students in rural, urban and suburban high schools, as well as community college. He has served as an independent counselor and is one of the counselors who assists students through the *Ask the Counselor* column on *MyFootpath.com*.

Patrick has served as President of the Michigan Association for College Admission Counseling and the National Association for College Admission Counseling. He is a recipient of the Outstanding Faculty Award from Oakland Community College, the Margaret Addis Service to NACAC Award, and the William Gramenz Award (for outstanding contributions to college counseling in Michigan). He holds five college degrees, including a Ph.D. in Education Administration.

Patrick lives with his wife and children in suburban Detroit.